D0711194

SUMMARY:

12 Rules for Life by Jordan B. Peterson

In A Nutshell Publications

Copyright © 2018 In A Nutshell Publications. Please note this is an UNOFFICIAL summary and analysis. This summary and analysis is not affiliated, authorized, approved, licensed, or endorsed by the subject book's author or publisher. All Rights Reserved. The publisher and author make no warranties or representations with respect to the accuracy or completeness of the contents of this book and specifically disclaim any implied warranties of merchantability or fitness for a particular purpose. Content and price subject to change without notice.

Table of Contents

Chapter One:

Rule 1 – Stand Up Straight with Your Shoulders Back

Peterson begins by describing how certain creatures have managed to develop techniques to protect their territory and enhance their chances of survival. He explains how male lobsters fight to establish dominance on the ocean floor, and how a wren aggressively puts up a fight to keep other birds away from its territory.

His conclusion from all this is simple - the fight over shelter, food, and mates is a life and death situation. In reality, even the victor often suffers serious injuries that leave him vulnerable to other competitors. There simply has to be a way to make the fight shorter, or better yet, avoid a fight in the first place. According to Peterson, the only thing that can achieve this is the dominance hierarchy.

He goes ahead to explain how defeat and victory have an impact on brain chemistry. The brain of a winner tends to produce high levels of serotonin and low levels of octopamine, while losers produce more octopamine than serotonin. Serotonin gives the winner an upright, confident posture that makes them appear taller and more dangerous. The octopamine makes losers appear defeated, inhibited, and sulking.

Peterson's point is that winning and losing the game of life alters brain chemistry in such a way that the physique is ultimately transformed. Those who project confidence then end up occupying higher levels in the pecking order and get all the best that life has to offer. On the other hand, those who lose begin to take on a more submissive posture and consequently move down the pecking order. In other words, when two creatures compete for resources, the dominant one will simply intimidate the other into submission, with no need for a long, drawn-out fight. Thus the cycle of victory and defeat continues.

Peterson then takes us on an evolutionary journey, explaining how the dominance hierarchy has been around for millions of years. We are all controlled by the section of our brain that monitors where we stand in the dominance hierarchy. When we experience defeat in life, our posture droops, we feel weak, and we easily fall into depression. This makes us easy targets for bullies who are higher up in the pecking order.

Every defeat we face lowers our serotonin levels even further, and this leads to less confidence, more stress and pain, less happiness, more illness, and a reduced lifespan. It doesn't even matter how much money you make. A person at the bottom of the dominance ladder is more likely to spend their money on alcohol and drugs since they rarely have the chance of experiencing pleasure.

Peterson emphasizes the key role that our brain plays in the dominance hierarchy. When people treat us with little respect, our brain notices this and automatically assigns us a lowly position and thus limits production of serotonin. This makes us hyper-responsive and constantly anticipating a series of negative events. Depression leads to feelings of low self-worth, which leads to withdrawal from family and friends. This withdrawal leads to isolation, which then makes us feel useless and withdraw even further. Ultimately, we get trapped in a positive feedback loop.

The worst thing about it is that this state of mind can follow us from childhood into adulthood. An adult who experienced childhood bullying and trauma may be successful in life, but the subconscious adaptations to their former life still remain. They will still experience unnecessary stress and uncertainty,

—

and their constant submissiveness will continue to attract negative attention from adult bullies.

Peterson wants us to realize a very important truth. We should never let others push us around, because this creates tyrannical societies where oppression is allowed to thrive. We all have the capacity to display aggression, but we must learn to channel this anger in a way that balances power and limits authoritarianism.

Just because a person is considered a loser by society doesn't mean they should continue living like one. We can overcome this posture of constant submissiveness caused by bullying, rejection, or trauma. All we need to do is change our body language by projecting a confident stance – back straight, shoulders pushed back, chest out, and head held high. You will look like a winner, people will treat you better, and your brain will produce more serotonin. You will climb the dominance hierarchy!

But Peterson also clarifies that it's not only about physical posture. We must also be bold in a spiritual or metaphysical sense. We must speak our minds and let others know that we too have rights that we are willing to fight for. That way, we will be taken seriously and be seen as competent. Thus we will ultimately find joy and meaning in our lives.

Key Takeaways:

- The dominance hierarchy is true for both animals and humans.

- Bad posture makes us an easy target for bullies higher up on the dominance ladder.

- We should never allow others to push us around, we all have the capacity to display controlled aggression.

- Stand straight up with your shoulders back.

- It isn't only about physical posture. We must also be bold in a spiritual or metaphysical sense. We must speak our minds and let others know that we too have rights that we are willing to fight for.

Chapter Two:

Rule 2 – Treat Yourself Like Someone You Are Responsible for Helping

What would make a person knowingly refuse to take life-saving drugs despite the impact it would have on their health? This is the question that Peterson wants us to contemplate. He explains that many patients receive prescriptions but don't fill them, skip their doses, or stop taking the medication altogether. This is such a rampant problem that Peterson implores us to investigate why we behave in such a self-loathing manner.

The strange thing is that if it were our pet dog that was sick, we would not hesitate to make sure that they received the best care possible. We would take them to the vet and go to great lengths to administer their drugs day and night. We appear to love our pets more than we do ourselves. But why can't we be as committed to ourselves as we are to others? Surely, there must be some kind of shame that is behind all this. To find the source of this shame, Peterson takes us back in time to the biblical Book of Genesis.

In today's world, we tend to be very scientific in our thinking. However, scientific truths only go back a mere 500 years. Before scientific perspectives were developed, we viewed reality very differently. For this reason, Peterson refers to the Bible as a way of answering this fundamental question.

In the book of Genesis, we have the story of Adam and Eve in the Garden of Eden. When God created the first man, Adam, He specifically asked him not to eat from the Tree of the Knowledge of Good and Evil. As the story goes, Adam and Eve weren't very conscious or self-conscious at first, despite the fact that they were totally naked.

A snake, symbolizing Satan or the Spirit of Evil, appeared before Eve and tempted her into eating the forbidden fruit from the Tree of the Knowledge of Good and Evil. Eve instantly became self-conscious. She then gave the fruit to Adam who also became self-conscious. For the first time in their lives, Adam and Eve realized that they were naked, and this caused them great shame.

Being naked is symbolic of being vulnerable, unprotected, and open to judgment. When we are ashamed, our flaws stand out for all to see, and this makes us feel unworthy. This is why Adam and Eve hid in the bushes when they heard God approaching them. They were afraid that God would see their flaws and judge them.

Peterson explains that vulnerable people are always afraid of telling the truth and feel unworthy to walk with God. When God asked Adam why he had partaken of the forbidden fruit, he immediately accused both Eve and God Himself. Eve accused the snake. God banished them from the Garden of Eden and condemned them to a life of pain and hard work.

So why do we treat ourselves with such self-loathing? The truth is that deep down in our subconscious, we see ourselves as naked, shameful, worthless, resentful, accusatory, and cowardly descendants of Adam. We feel that we do not deserve to be treated well, and so we hold ourselves in contempt. We believe that even our dogs deserve better than us.

Peterson points out that it is our self-consciousness that makes us do cruel and evil things. Animals do not have this capacity. Due to Adam and Eve's Original Sin, we now know just how vile our intentions and actions can be, and this knowledge of good and evil secretly makes us hate ourselves.

But there is hope!

If we are to take better care of and respect ourselves, we must live and speak the Truth. If we begin to speak the Truth, we would shed the shackles of shame and walk with God again. This is how we would regain our self-respect and treat ourselves just like we treat those we care for.

Key Takeaways:

- Many of us behave in a self-destructive, self-loathing manner.

- Why? Peterson takes us back to the story of Adam and Eve. The end results being that deep down in our subconscious, we see ourselves as naked, shameful, worthless, resentful, accusatory, and cowardly descendants of Adam.

- To combat this, we must begin to speak the truth.

- We can shed the shackles of shame and regain our self-respect by treating ourselves just like we treat those we care for.

Chapter Three:

Rule 3 – Make Friends with People Who Want the Best for You

Peterson starts by telling a story of his childhood experiences in Alberta, Canada. He narrates how he and his friends Chris and Ed spent their teenage years driving around town and getting wasted at house parties. Due to peer pressure, engaging in all kinds of risky behaviors was the order of the day. For some reason, his friends always seemed to gravitate toward the worst parts of town.

He talks about how all of his friends dropped out of high school and he began associating with a different group of students. In college, he met like-minded companions who motivated and inspired him to create a better life for himself. Peterson had managed to break free from his past.

However, his former friends weren't so lucky or willing to do so. Ed was still hanging out with friends who were constantly stoned. Years later, Chris committed suicide after suffering a psychotic break probably caused by drug abuse.

Peterson invites us to consider why his former companions Chris and Ed found it so difficult to leave their bad friendships behind and improve their lives. This is a phenomenon that is quite common in society. Some continually choose to associate with people and places that bring them down instead of raising them up.

According to Peterson, there are a number of reasons why we do this. One of them is a refusal to accept responsibility for our lives. We keep picking friends that remind us of our negative past, maybe because we have a low opinion of ourselves. We simply don't believe that we deserve better friends. Freud referred to this as *"repetition compulsion,"* where we use the same faulty tools to create the same faulty results we have become accustomed to.

Another reason is that we often want to feel like saviors or superheroes, so we try to rescue others who seem like victims. Peterson reminds us that not everyone who fails qualifies as a victim. Some people have made a conscious decision to accept their suffering and are simply looking to exploit the generosity of others. Our attempt to save them simply causes us to lower our own standards.

Peterson emphasizes this argument clearly. He asks us to imagine a troubled employee who is introduced to a team of excellent and diligent workers. The supervisor believes that the troubled employee will learn from his brilliant teammates and thus be inspired to improve his work ethic.

Unfortunately, the reverse happens, and the whole team degenerates into mediocrity. The troubled employee infects the team with his cynicism, arrogance, and poor work ethic. The teammates conclude that there is no reason to perform well when the new team member isn't pulling his weight. From this example, Peterson shows us how, in an attempt to help someone, we may end up spreading delinquency. It is simply easier for us to copy bad behavior that drags us down than mimic good behavior that lifts us up.

We tend to hang around bad friends because it is easier. We don't talk about the way we are negatively influencing each other, but everyone in the group understands that we are all headed downhill. Nobody wants to confront the real issue. Moving up in life is difficult, so before we jump in and try to help others, we should find out whether the person is an actual victim of circumstance or if they have refused to accept responsibility for their life. We might discover that some of our so-called friends are simply taking advantage of us and want to drag us down to their level.

Peterson asks us to look closely at our friends and see whether we are using loyalty as an excuse for associating with people who don't want what's best for us. After all, loyalty should never be equated to stupidity.

Find people who will support you on your way up, inspire you to do well, and hold you accountable when you start to lose focus.

Key Takeaways:

- You are the average of the five people you spend most time with.

- Stop trying to 'rescue' people who don't deserve to be rescued.

- In an attempt to help someone, we may end up spreading delinquency.

- Of course we should still help people, but before jumping in take a moment to decide if the person is an actual victim of circumstance or if they have refused to accept responsibility for their life.

- Ideally, your friends will support you on your way up, inspire you to do well, and hold you accountable when you start to lose focus.

Chapter Four:

Rule 4 – Compare Yourself to Who You Were Yesterday, not to Who Someone Else Is Today

In today's world of seven billion people where everyone is connected digitally, it is very difficult to claim that you are the best at something. There will always be someone out there who can perform better than you. Peterson reminds us that this is a reality we are all subconsciously aware of.

This has created a culture where the winners get access to more resources than those at the bottom of the ladder. The result is widespread dissatisfaction and feelings of worthlessness. That internal critic keeps telling us that we will never be as successful as other people. In an attempt to counter this negative mental state, social psychologists have been telling us for decades to create lies to make ourselves feel better.

However, Peterson recommends that we look at this game of life differently and stop listening to our internal critic. Every activity has a chance of success or failure. We can do something better or worse; otherwise, there would be no point in doing it. Yet our inner critic keeps telling us that we aren't good enough, so we must find a way to silence this voice. The first step is to redefine what we mean by success and failure. We have been led to believe that it is either one or the other; with no middle ground or alternatives. But the truth is that success and failure lie on a continuum that has degrees and gradations.

He asks us to consider life as a series of games instead of a singular one. We need to find the game that matches our talents and strengths and work on it. Why should you be jealous of your coworker who is a consistent performer at work yet his wife is cheating on him? Why envy a wealthy celebrity who is a bigot and alcoholic? The problem we have is that we pick one area of life and compare ourselves to others in that specific area. We end up overvaluing what we lack and undervaluing what we do.

Instead of trying to beat everybody at everything, we should be focusing on growing our talents over time. Every individual is unique in their own way, so there's no need to compare ourselves to others. We should learn to identify what to pursue and what to let go.

Peterson explains that with the limited resources we have in our lives, we should pay attention to the things that matter most to us. Trying to chase after everything you see will deplete your energy and leave you dissatisfied when you fail to meet your lofty goals.

At the end of the day, we should all aim for the highest good and seek self-improvement instead of defining our success by world standards.

Key Takeaways:

- Aim to better yourself, without comparing to others.

- Success and failure are not as definite as we are led to believe, there is a gradient for both.

- Life is a series of games, not just a singular one.

- Pay attention only to the things that matter most to you.

Chapter Five:

Rule 5 - Do Not Let Your Children Do Anything That Makes You Dislike Them

Parenting is a tough job, and every parent has their own style of disciplining their kids. However, there are some behaviors and attitudes that no parent should ever tolerate. Peterson gives some instances where he witnessed children getting out of control in public and parents too helpless to do anything about it. If we allow our kids to develop behaviors that we hate, why should we think that other people will want to be around such an individual?

Peterson argues that parents need to take the time to teach their kids how to behave, especially in public, so that they do not become an embarrassment to society. By giving your child too much freedom to do or say whatever they want, you are robbing them of the opportunity to become an independent person. There are times when kids simply need to hear a firm "No," regardless of how much you love them.

Sometimes it's not too much love that stifles the development of a child. It's neglect. Peterson gives the example of a four-year-old boy who wouldn't eat anything the whole day, and his mother, who happened to be a psychologist, didn't even care enough to find out what the problem was. Unconscious hatred for a child can also turn them into misbehaved or damaged members of society.

In today's society, we have this perception that it's the parents who should be blamed when kids behave badly. Peterson argues that this naïve notion of children being angels who should not be held responsible for their bad behavior is dangerous. This notion avoids the fact that every individual has some level of corruption within them. Otherwise, where did the corruption we see in society come from?

According to Peterson, it is illogical to expect society as a whole to restructure itself to suit the behavior of an individual. We do not need to solve one person's private troubles by implementing a social revolution. It is Rousseau who came up with the idea that all children have pure spirits that are ultimately corrupted by societal culture. If this is so, why do we become more disciplined and well-behaved as we age?

Furthermore, we cannot blame human society or culture as being the source of corruption. Even chimpanzees are known to roam around in gangs, brutally beating and killing any stranger that doesn't belong to their tribe.

The truth is that children will not become good members of society if we simply leave them to make their own decisions. They need to be socialized so that they fit in. Though we aren't perfect, socialization doesn't harm kids as much as it disciplines and helps them thrive. When kids demand attention from their parents, it is a sign that they are trying to become part of a broader community, which is a very necessary thing if you want to get along with others.

Peterson explains that most modern parents want to act like friends to their children, which then makes them fearful of chastising or punishing them for bad behavior. We forget that as a friend, you cannot authoritatively discipline your child. If the child hates you for a little while, so be it. But if we do not properly teach our children how to behave, they will not be able to interact with society in a meaningful and productive way.

We need to realize that kids refuse to listen to their parents because they want to dominate the relationship. If we let them, they will never respect any adult they interact with. Even when a child cries after being disciplined, it is mostly due to anger and not sadness or fear. Knowing this can help parents take control of the situation and enforce proper rules. Peterson gives us five principles for proper parenting. The first is to limit the number of rules we give our children so that we don't overburden them. The second is to use minimum force when disciplining children. The third is that parenting is most effective when done by a couple instead of a single parent. The fourth is that we need to avoid being resentful and vengeful when our children misbehave. Finally, every parent needs to realize that their primary responsibility isn't to make their children happy. It is to ensure that they grow into socially desirable members of society.

Key Takeaways:

- Children need to be socialized so that they fit and are desirable members of society.

- A parents' primary aim should not be to become friends with their children as this will not allow for proper discipline when it is required.

- Follow Petersons' five principles for proper parenting.

Chapter Six:

Rule 6 - Set Your House in Perfect Order Before You Criticize the World

The sentiments of the people who commit mass murders paint a very telling picture of how most of humanity views life. If we look at the Sandy Hook, Columbine, and Colorado theater shooters, we can see that these killers all failed to cope with the realities of life. Peterson recollects how one of the Columbine killers wrote about humanity being contemptible and life being harsh and unfair. By criticizing the world, these mass murderers decided to become supreme judges of human reality.

The truth is that life is hard, painful, and full of suffering. People simply choose to cope differently with what life offers. Some ignore these problems. Others bury their problems in excessive hedonism. Another group decides to keep forging ahead regardless. However, there are those who choose to destroy themselves and others as a form of protest against what they consider a meaningless and evil life.

Peterson asks us to consider how and why people suffer great injustices but end up responding to their experiences in totally different ways. He discusses the lives of people like Cain in the Bible and Carl Panzram. Due to a feeling of rejection by God, Cain chose to kill his brother, Abel, in a jealous rage. Carl Pazram also went through immense torture and rape in a juvenile institution, and he ended up a burglar, rapist, arsonist, and serial killer.

Then Peterson contrasts this first group with individuals like Aleksandr Solzhenitsyn, Mahatma Gandhi, Vaclav Havel, and even some of his own clients who all managed to overcome terrible torment and abuse to turn their world around.

We all know that the world is corrupt and evil, but the problem with criticizing the world is that it makes us feel powerless to change our lives. If we allow a desire for vengeance to take root, sooner or later we will feel compelled to act out against the people around us. Peterson reminds us that vengeance, bitterness, and blaming God only prevents us from engaging in productive thoughts to make our lives better. If we do not accept responsibility for the terrible sufferings that we face, then surely we are all doomed to a life of misery.

He offers a solution to this miserable reality. He concludes that we all need to clean up our lives. We can start in small ways. We need to stop engaging in things we know are wrong. We must start treating others better and take care of our health. We should work hard and take advantage of every opportunity we come by instead of complaining about the world system being flawed. Simple everyday acts that will build up over time to change the way you perceive your world.

Life will still be full of inevitable tragedies, but at least your soul will not be encumbered with bitterness and anger. If everyone allowed their soul to guide them, this world wouldn't be as corrupt and evil as it is today. But as long as we focus more on blaming the world for all our tragedies instead of looking inward at our own faults, we will never achieve any meaningful results.

Key Takeaways:

- Life will not always be happy, we all must go through pain and suffering. It helps to realize this and face up to our problems instead of escaping them.

- Start with small actions and stop engaging in things that are wrong.

- We may not be able to change the world but we can always look inwards and change ourselves.

Chapter Seven:

Rule 7 – Pursue What Is Meaningful (Not What Is Expedient)

Life is full of suffering. This is the message that God delivered to Adam and Eve when he told them that henceforth they would have to work, sweat, and sacrifice to eat. In essence, this was a curse. But does this mean that the only way to counter this toil is to live impulsively, pursue pleasure, and do whatever we want as long as we don't get caught?

We need to consider whether there is a better way to live apart from chasing fleeting pleasures. Peterson again offers a biblical perspective where people were required to offer sacrifices to God to gain His favor. His premise is that by sacrificing what we have today, we can gain something valuable in the future. Sacrifice and work is practically the same thing, and both these things point to a delay of gratification.

Peterson puts forth two critical questions. The first one is "What exactly must we sacrifice?" Small sacrifices only solve small problems and vice versa. Therefore, if we want to secure a better future, we must be prepared to make big sacrifices today.

The second question is "What are the limits of the sacrifice if it is to be most effective?" Using the biblical narrative of Cain and Abel, Peterson shows us that not all sacrifices are of the same quality. For a sacrifice to be of high quality, it must cost you so much that it would be painful to let go of. He points to the ultimate sacrifice that Christ made on the cross for the redemption of all mankind. This kind of sacrifice is the only way to keep the world's pain and suffering at bay.

Deep down, we all know that great sacrifices will help us do more good in this world than expediency ever will. The problem is that most of us don't want to adopt this approach. We can argue that Christ was the son of God, but Peterson uses the example of Socrates to show that it is possible to willingly pay the ultimate price to ensure a life of meaning and truth. From Socrates, we learn that by rejecting expediency and living according to our highest ideals, we can overcome even the fear of death.

According to Peterson, it is our self-consciousness that

produces suffering, which then motivates us toward expediency and immediate gratification. However, we can keep suffering at bay by choosing to sacrifice. But is a tragedy the primary and only source of our suffering? No, it is not. Evil is a bigger source of suffering.

Evil came into the world through self-consciousness. Before Adam and Eve's eyes were opened by eating the forbidden fruit, there was no such thing as evil. Therefore, the biggest problem we face isn't just sacrificing to avoid suffering. We must also contemplate what and how to sacrifice to reduce evil in the world. Peterson explains that diminishing evil is not something simple. There is only one solution that has ever worked, and it came in the form of Jesus Christ.

He elaborates how Christ represents the highest ideal of all mankind. We all want to achieve the higher good and create heaven on earth, but we have to contend with evil. If Christ resisted the three temptations of instant gratification offered by Satan himself, so must we. If the highest good is found in Christ, then we must take on His nature, make the right sacrifices, and avoid chasing after temporary pleasures.

This is how we live a life of meaning. Act today in a manner that will benefit you, your family, and the world for many years to come.

Key Takeaways:

- Sacrifice and work are practically the same thing.

- To achieve anything meanwhile we have to sacrifice. Usually the bigger the sacrifice the bigger the reward.

- Resist evil. Make the right sacrifices and avoid chasing after temporary pleasures.

Chapter Eight:

Rule 8 – Tell the Truth, or at Least Don't Lie

In life, we have the choice of telling the truth, no matter how awful it may sound, or taking the easy way out and lying. Peterson presents these two paths as totally different ways of life.

We have the tendency to manipulate the world around us to get what we desire. We flatter, scheme, and use propaganda to please ourselves or others. We engage in what Sigmund Freud referred to as "life-lies." These are the lies we tell when we are trying to replace reality with perception to create a predefined outcome. According to Peterson, there are two premises for living such a lie.

The first is that we believe the knowledge we currently possess is enough to define a better future for us. However, there is no justification for this because what we may be aiming for may not be of value or our current knowledge may be erroneous. The second premise is that if we allow life to play out on its own, life will be unbearable. This is not true because life is not inherently intolerable. The problem here is that we create a false sense of reality and then try to actualize it. This is a form of pride.

Peterson talks about life-lies that are founded on avoidance. Most people believe that sins of commission, where you knowingly do something that is wrong, are much worse than sins of omission, where you keep silent when bad things are happening instead of taking action. Peterson disagrees with this notion.

He argues that when we avoid conflict, allow people to mistreat us, and try to remain invisible, we are slowly obliterating all meaning from our lives. Avoidance makes us sick slaves who suffer because we never get what we need from life. We fail to reveal our true selves to others and consequently, never get to know ourselves. This creates an incomplete life.

We need to understand that falsehoods do not improve our reality. You can keep quiet today and choose to go along with tyranny, but soon enough you will be forced to do things you never thought you were capable of.

Peterson explains how willful blindness is the worst type of lie. This occurs when you refuse to acknowledge the obvious or admit that your plan contains errors. Willful blindness is dangerous because it is subtle and easily rationalized. When something goes wrong and you fail, you blame everything and everyone except yourself. You become bitter and seek ways of getting back at the world.

The Soviet states are used to describe how citizens willingly chose to live a lie every day by denying the fact that their government was oppressing them and causing them untold suffering. Avoidance of truth and living in denial can make us unwitting perpetrators of the worst crimes imaginable. Peterson makes the case that the rational mind has the capacity to deceive and manipulate anyone, so we shouldn't depend on reason alone. Reason will tell you that you already know everything and there is no need to confront your inner Being. Reason will convince you that your theories are absolute truths and you should have faith in the known. This is precisely the same temptation that befell Lucifer right before he rebelled against God. Reason breeds totalitarianism, and totalitarianism will promise you a Utopia that will never materialize. A totalitarian will never stop to ask whether their goals are flawed. Their ambition becomes their god.

The only hope we have is to be willing to learn from what we do not know. We need to stop lying to ourselves and admit we don't know the whole truth. We must set goals that will ensure we grow in character and ability instead of trying to manipulate our way toward power, money, and status. When adversity strikes, the only thing that will get you through is your character.

When we are truthful to ourselves, we seek information that allows our goal to transform. Truth nourishes the soul and prevents us from turning into vengeful people who are constantly blaming the world. If we only told the truth, no matter what, the world would be a Paradise.

Key Takeaways:

- We always have the choice to tell the truth.

- Omission is just as bad as commission when it comes to lying. Trying to remain invisible will slowly obliterate all meaning from life.

- Willful blindness is the worst type of lie and should be avoided at all costs.

- We must focus on growing in character and staying true. When adversity strikes, only character will get you through.

Chapter Nine:

Rule 9 – Assume That the Person You Are Listening to Might Know Something You Don't

Peterson begins by explaining the difference between psychotherapy and advice. He says that when someone gives you advice about a complex situation you are in, they are simply looking for a way to shut you up and move on to more interesting matters. Psychotherapy, however, is a real conversation where both parties listen and talk to each other, and come up with strategies for solving their problems. Talking is actually a way of engaging our thinking processes. Peterson argues that most of us rarely think or listen. What we call thinking is actually self-criticism. For us to engage in genuine thinking, we have to create a dialogue between two people in our minds. There has to be a speaker and a listener who provide different viewpoints. This internal conflict is what then makes us good listeners.

Peterson describes how Freud used to face away from his patients to avoid influencing them with his facial expressions. But Peterson believes that being a good psychotherapist means creating a personal relationship with people. The Freudian approach creates distance and the patient only ends up receiving advice. However, the personal approach creates an atmosphere where both therapist and patient listen to each other. He advises us to learn how to listen in a subtle manner that sometimes involves responding with facial expressions instead of words.

The problem we have today is that most of us are not bold enough to listen to what others are saying. We would rather evaluate people's words. The best way to practice good listening is to first summarize what the other person has said before expressing your viewpoint. If they agree with your summary, then you state your opinion.

This is beneficial because you will gain a genuine understanding of what the person has said. The second benefit is that it helps the other person distill and consolidate their memory, thus making the conversation better. Finally, it prevents you from offering weak, oversimplified, or distorted arguments designed to harm the other person's position.

Listening attentively gives the speaker time to formulate their ideas and flesh out their point. By listening without expressing any premature judgment, you allow people to open up and truthfully tell you their side of the story. This is what makes conversations interesting. Peterson states that whenever we find a conversation boring, it's because we aren't truly listening.

Though talking is part of thinking, this isn't always the case. There are some conversations where people jockey for position in the dominance hierarchy. One person says something interesting and the other tries to top it. Another example is when two people talk but nobody is listening to the other. When it's your turn to speak, you end up saying something totally off-topic and the conversation ends abruptly.

There are also conversations where a person is more focused on winning the argument rather than being right. This occurs when you ridicule others ideas, provide selective evidence, or try to impress your supporters. This is what happens in political and economic debates.

Peterson defines a genuine listening conversation as one where everyone listens and only one person speaks at a time. We should focus on learning from others instead of justifying our fixed positions. Genuine listening conversations allow us to declutter and organize our minds. At the end of the day, listening will bring about transformation in our lives.

Key Takeaways:

- For us to engage in genuine thinking, we have to create a dialogue between two people in our minds.

- The best way to practice good listening is to first summarize what the other person has said before expressing your viewpoint.

- By listening without expressing any premature judgment, you allow people to open up and truthfully tell you their side of the story.

- We should focus on learning from others instead of justifying our fixed positions.

Chapter Ten:

Rule 10 – Be Precise in Your Speech

The world around us is a complex system of interconnected objects. Peterson explains that we tend to reduce this complexity down to something that fits our purpose. This is the only way to make sense of the world.

Instead of seeing an entity, we perceive its direct meaning. Floors aren't just floors; they are surfaces to walk on. Chairs are for sitting. Rocks are for throwing. When we talk to people, we don't see cells and molecules; we see facial expressions that generate a rapport. In essence, we only focus on the attributes that help us plan our lives and achieve our goals. All this is viewed within a narrow window of time. If we tried to perceive all the individual objects within the context of yesterday and tomorrow instead of just right now, we would go insane.

Peterson argues that we need to perceive the functional utility of things around us so that life becomes simple for us to understand. If we do not become precise in our goals, we will be overwhelmed by the complex nature of our world. With all the chaos we have in our interconnected world, it can be extremely difficult to make sense of it all.

If you are driving a car, you don't really perceive all the individual parts or the entire object itself. All you care about is whether it gets you from one place to another. It is only when your car suddenly stops working that you begin to think about how complex the entire system is. Your incompetence is thus revealed.

It is only during crisis or failure that we realize how limited our perception and understanding is. When we fail to specify things with precision, chaos comes in and changes everything we thought we knew. Our carelessness and ignorance are exposed, and we begin to understand what precision has been protecting us from.

Peterson uses the example of a loyal wife who learns that her hard-working, reliable, and loving husband has been spending his long "working hours" with another woman. He explains how the wife's perception of her husband is instantly destroyed and she begins to doubt everything else in her life. Chaos generally emerges when we refuse to communicate in a precise way. We are too scared of admitting the terrible emotions we harbor in our souls, so we sweep things under the rug. In due time, every conversation that went unsaid accumulates and produces resentment and bitterness. Even when we perceive problems arising, we convince ourselves that peace is the best solution. So we keep quiet and avoid taking responsibility.

By refusing to confront minor issues, we allow them to grow and swallow the ordered lives we lead. We end up with suffering and confusion. According to Peterson, the solution is to find the precise words to use when communicating with others. Courage and honesty are required to ensure that our reality maintains its simple and well-defined order.

Every difficult conversation must be defined so that the topic becomes specific to that particular point in time. Couples usually stop communicating because every argument moves away from the present problem and into past and future transgressions. Our minds cannot handle a conversation that covers everything we have ever done or might do. We must focus on specific things and use precise speech to get our message across.

By paying attention to the words we use, we will discover that sometimes we are wrong and it is our perceptions that need to change. Once we correct our errors, we will add meaning to our lives and move toward a specified destination.

Key Takeaways:

- If we do not become precise in our goals, we will be overwhelmed by the complex nature of our world.

- Chaos generally emerges when we refuse to communicate in a precise way.

- When problems arise, keeping quiet and aiming for peace is not the best solution.

- The solution is to find the precise words to use when communicating with others. Courage and honesty are required for this as it can be scary to admit the terrible emotions we keep locked away.

Chapter Eleven:

Rule 11 – Do Not Bother Children When They Are Skateboarding

There is a certain level of risk that humans desire in their day-to-day activities. Peterson uses the example of safe playgrounds to highlight this fact. If something is made too safe, or if an activity like skateboarding is restricted, we find other risky things to do. We seem to enjoy living on the edge, though this is true for some more than others. Without the feeling of excitement that risk creates, we become dull and careless beings who are overprotected and thus unprepared when unexpected danger strikes.

According to Peterson, the human spirit thrives in danger. Anyone who tries to establish too many rules under the guise of "protecting" people from risky activities is simply being sinister and anti-human. By examining the consequences of an action, we can conclude the motivation of the person who committed the act. Those who advocated for socialism didn't do so because they loved the poor. They simply hated rich people. This explains why the poor suffered the most under socialism.

Some of the feats we are accomplishing today would have been considered impossible and too dangerous 50 years ago. The records that have been broken in sports and the creation of extreme sports all indicate that humanity doesn't have any real limits. However, there are those who have chosen to look at humanity as a stain that must be eliminated from the planet. They believe that we have polluted and defiled the earth. Peterson believes that this paradigm has affected the mental health of boys because the male species is blamed for things like the rape culture and plundering the planet. This has led to terrible consequences.

Peterson explains how boys in today's world are suffering. Boys are naturally more competitive, more daring, and less agreeable than girls. Girls are allowed to compete with fellow girls as well as boys, and it won't even matter when they lose to their male counterparts. But boys who engage in girl games or compete against girls are frowned upon. If the boy wins, he is being unfair. If he loses to a girl, he's weak. This forces boys to engage in purely male-dominated activities, where you are expected to challenge authority and fight for status.

Statistics show that the number of girls attending universities is increasing at a faster rate than that of boys. Peterson foresees a time when women will dominate the majority of university courses, and the number of men will drop even further. This is bad news both for men and women. Women desire to date and marry men who are of equal or greater educational or economic status. With fewer men seeking university education and more men becoming unemployed, women are getting frustrated. Surprisingly, marriage is now becoming a preserve for the rich.

Peterson argues that part of the problem is the political correctness in universities. Men have been painted as perpetrators of an oppressive system meant to exclude women. Yet we forget that men have played a major role in freeing women from drudgery throughout history without personal gain being the primary motivation. Inventions such as chloroform for childbirth and low-cost tampons are just two examples of the dedication of men to female causes. Trying to socialize boys to behave more like girls is having terrible consequences for both genders. Society may give the impression that a man's aggressive, competitive, and risk-taking nature is the cause of all our problems, but the truth is that women want men who are independent, tough, and stable.

If men are pushed to become soft and harmless, they begin to veer in the extreme direction. Weak men are more capable of committing heinous crimes than tough guys. Peterson concludes that we should allow boys to go through the process of becoming men. It may involve a lot of aggressive games and risky behavior, but these dangerous acts are what ultimately make men strong.

Key Takeaways:

- We need a certain amount of risk to make life exciting.

- Boys are expected to engage in purely male-dominated activities.

- The number of males attending university is decreasing while the number of females is increasing, this is bad news in the long run.

- Women want men who are of equal or greater educational or economic status.

- If men are pushed to become soft and harmless, they begin to veer in the extreme direction and become undesirable.

- Boys should be allowed to go through the process of becoming men, there may be risks but ultimately they will become strong.

Chapter Twelve:

Rule 12 – Pet a Cat When You Encounter One On the Street

All world religions believe that suffering is a key component of life. There are so many things that happen to people every day that cause immense pain and suffering. Peterson narrates his experience when his children became sick at a young age. He contemplated just how limited and vulnerable we are as human beings, with diseases and tragedies striking us at every turn.

Sometimes we find it difficult to understand why God, the creator of this world, allows such suffering to occur. Peterson explains how he wished he could change his son into a being that could resist all kinds of suffering. Unfortunately, this would turn his son into a robot. We need to realize that strengthening ourselves against all suffering may remove our limitations, but we will ultimately lose that which makes us human. If we are no longer fragile beings, then we also stop being lovable and loving.

Whenever we experience tragedy, we wonder why it had to be us. Peterson argues that our vulnerability helps us to grow. If suddenly we had everything we need, the story of life would cease to exist. There would be no story and life would be very boring.

Peterson uses the example of the original comic superhero, Superman, who had a few specific powers. Decades later, the writers gave him more powers that made him invulnerable. Suddenly, the Superman storyline became boring because nothing could hurt him. They had to introduce kryptonite to make Superman compelling to the audience.

We love to see or hear stories of people who faced great limitations and overcame them to better their lives. With no vulnerabilities, we won't have anything to fight for or against, and we would lead static lives with no genuine growth. Only entities that have limitations can become something greater than they are today.

This doesn't mean that we should accept unnecessary suffering. However, giving up on life and humanity as a whole is not the answer. Those who choose suicide or mass murder just because they don't agree with the suffering they see in today's world are simply making a terrible situation worse. By hating life and the pain that comes with it, we perpetuate the very same evil we are trying to withstand. But with all the horrors of our existence, what alternative do we have?

According to Peterson, this question cannot be answered by thinking. If thinking was the answer, then the great minds throughout history would have found an answer to the world's suffering by now. When something intolerable happens, all our thinking faculties go out the window. He believes that when things go wrong, we need to *notice*, not think.

We must notice the good in people and situations around us even when we are going through painful experiences. When two people are in love, they don't love each other *in spite of* their limitations, but *because of* their limitations. Of course, you can work on some of the limitations, but you must accept that some things cannot be improved beyond a certain point. Peterson gives us insight on how he coped with the overwhelming medical challenges his daughter faced. He advises us to spend time talking and thinking about how the crisis will be managed every day. We must develop a plan for the future to limit the impact of the suffering. We need to see the situation as a war instead of a battle to avoid fighting too hard and burning out. Finally, we need to have faith in God and focus on improving the things we can control.

Despite our weaknesses, humans are tough and able to survive the pain and loss life brings. The only way to persevere is to believe that life is ultimately a good thing. We should notice the small opportunities for happiness that life brings our way every day, no matter how bad things get. For just a few moments, we can be reminded that life is a wonderful experience, despite the suffering that exists.

Key Takeaways:

- If suddenly we had everything we need, the story of life would cease to exist and become very boring.

- Only through having limitations can we become something greater than we are today.

- When crisis occurs, we need to plan how the crisis will be managed every day. We must develop a plan and see the issue as a war and not a battle to avoid burning out.

- The only way to persevere is to believe that life is ultimately a good thing. We should notice the small opportunities for happiness that life brings our way every day.

Conclusion

This book is a treasure trove of good advice. To ensure the lessons stick, I like to go over just the key takeaways at the end of each chapter once a week. I do this for this book and all the other summaries I've wrote to ensure the key principles are really engrained into my mind and soon become natural habits and reactions in my every day life.

Thanks for checking out my book. I hope you found this of value and enjoyed it. But before you go, I have one small favor to ask...

Would you take 60 seconds and write a review about this book on Amazon?

Reviews are the best way for independent authors (like me) to get noticed, sell more books, and it gives me the motivation to continue producing. I also read every review and use the feedback to write future revisions – and even future books.

Thanks again.

23867352R00039

Made in the USA
Lexington, KY
17 December 2018